CHILD CARE RECEIPT

Child's Name : .... Date : ....

Received From : .... Amount : $ [____]

Paid By : ☐ Cash
☐ Check
☐ Credit Card

For child care services from : ....
To : ....

Balance Due $: ....
Providers EIN Or SSN : ....

Providers Signature : _____

CHILD CARE RECEIPT

Child's Name : .... Date : ....

Received From : .... Amount : $ [____]

Paid By : ☐ Cash
☐ Check
☐ Credit Card

For child care services from : ....
To : ....

Balance Due $: ....
Providers EIN Or SSN : ....

Providers Signature : _____

CHILD CARE RECEIPT

Child's Name : .... Date : ....

Received From : .... Amount : $ [____]

Paid By : ☐ Cash
☐ Check
☐ Credit Card

For child care services from : ....
To : ....

Balance Due $: ....
Providers EIN Or SSN : ....

Providers Signature : _____

D1318349

CHILD CARE
RECEIPT

Child's Name : .... Date : ....

Received From : ....

Amount : $ [____]

Paid By : ☐ Cash
☐ Check
☐ Credit Card

For child care services from : ....

To : ....

Balance Due $: ....

Providers EIN Or SSN : ....

Providers Signature :

CHILD CARE
RECEIPT

Child's Name : .... Date : ....

Received From : ....

Amount : $ [____]

Paid By : ☐ Cash
☐ Check
☐ Credit Card

For child care services from : ....

To : ....

Balance Due $: ....

Providers EIN Or SSN : ....

Providers Signature :

CHILD CARE
RECEIPT

Child's Name : .... Date : ....

Received From : ....

Amount : $ [____]

Paid By : ☐ Cash
☐ Check
☐ Credit Card

For child care services from : ....

To : ....

Balance Due $: ....

Providers EIN Or SSN : ....

Providers Signature :

CHILD CARE RECEIPT

Child's Name : .... Date : ....

Received From : ....

Amount : $ [   ]

Paid By : ☐ Cash
         ☐ Check
         ☐ Credit Card

For child care services from : ....
To : ....
Balance Due $: ....
Providers EIN Or SSN : ....

Providers Signature :

CHILD CARE RECEIPT

Child's Name : .... Date : ....

Received From : ....

Amount : $ [   ]

Paid By : ☐ Cash
         ☐ Check
         ☐ Credit Card

For child care services from : ....
To : ....
Balance Due $: ....
Providers EIN Or SSN : ....

Providers Signature :

CHILD CARE RECEIPT

Child's Name : .... Date : ....

Received From : ....

Amount : $ [   ]

Paid By : ☐ Cash
         ☐ Check
         ☐ Credit Card

For child care services from : ....
To : ....
Balance Due $: ....
Providers EIN Or SSN : ....

Providers Signature :

CHILD CARE RECEIPT

Child's Name : .... Date : ....

Received From : .... Amount : $ [   ]

For child care services from : ....

To : ....

Paid By : ☐ Cash
☐ Check
☐ Credit Card

Balance Due $: ....

Providers EIN Or SSN : ....

Providers Signature :

CHILD CARE RECEIPT

Child's Name : .... Date : ....

Received From : .... Amount : $ [   ]

For child care services from : ....

To : ....

Paid By : ☐ Cash
☐ Check
☐ Credit Card

Balance Due $: ....

Providers EIN Or SSN : ....

Providers Signature :

CHILD CARE RECEIPT

Child's Name : .... Date : ....

Received From : .... Amount : $ [   ]

For child care services from : ....

To : ....

Paid By : ☐ Cash
☐ Check
☐ Credit Card

Balance Due $: ....

Providers EIN Or SSN : ....

Providers Signature :

CHILD CARE RECEIPT

Child's Name : .... Date : ....

Received From : ....

Amount : $ [   ]

For child care services from : ....

Paid By : ☐ Cash
☐ Check
☐ Credit Card

To : ....

Balance Due $: ....

Providers EIN Or SSN : ....

Providers Signature :

CHILD CARE RECEIPT

Child's Name : .... Date : ....

Received From : ....

Amount : $ [   ]

For child care services from : ....

Paid By : ☐ Cash
☐ Check
☐ Credit Card

To : ....

Balance Due $: ....

Providers EIN Or SSN : ....

Providers Signature :

CHILD CARE RECEIPT

Child's Name : .... Date : ....

Received From : ....

Amount : $ [   ]

For child care services from : ....

Paid By : ☐ Cash
☐ Check
☐ Credit Card

To : ....

Balance Due $: ....

Providers EIN Or SSN : ....

Providers Signature :

CHILD CARE

RECEIPT

Child's Name : ....   Date : ....

Received From : ....

For child care services from : ....

To : ....

Balance Due $: ....

Providers EIN Or SSN : ....

Amount : $ [   ]

Paid By : ☐ Cash
          ☐ Check
          ☐ Credit Card

Providers Signature :

CHILD CARE

RECEIPT

Child's Name : ....   Date : ....

Received From : ....

For child care services from : ....

To : ....

Balance Due $: ....

Providers EIN Or SSN : ....

Amount : $ [   ]

Paid By : ☐ Cash
          ☐ Check
          ☐ Credit Card

Providers Signature :

CHILD CARE

RECEIPT

Child's Name : ....   Date : ....

Received From : ....

For child care services from : ....

To : ....

Balance Due $: ....

Providers EIN Or SSN : ....

Amount : $ [   ]

Paid By : ☐ Cash
          ☐ Check
          ☐ Credit Card

Providers Signature :

CHILD CARE RECEIPT

Child's Name : .... Date : ....

Received From : ....

For child care services from : ....
To : ....

Balance Due $: ....

Providers EIN Or SSN : ....

Providers Signature :

Amount : $ [   ]

Paid By : ☐ Cash
☐ Check
☐ Credit Card

CHILD CARE RECEIPT

Child's Name : .... Date : ....

Received From : ....

For child care services from : ....
To : ....

Balance Due $: ....

Providers EIN Or SSN : ....

Providers Signature :

Amount : $ [   ]

Paid By : ☐ Cash
☐ Check
☐ Credit Card

CHILD CARE RECEIPT

Child's Name : .... Date : ....

Received From : ....

For child care services from : ....
To : ....

Balance Due $: ....

Providers EIN Or SSN : ....

Providers Signature :

Amount : $ [   ]

Paid By : ☐ Cash
☐ Check
☐ Credit Card

CHILD CARE RECEIPT

Child's Name : .... Date : ....

Received From : ....

Amount : $ [   ]

Paid By : ☐ Cash
          ☐ Check
          ☐ Credit Card

For child care services from : ....
                          To : ....

Balance Due $: ....

Providers EIN Or SSN : ....

Providers Signature :

CHILD CARE RECEIPT

Child's Name : .... Date : ....

Received From : ....

Amount : $ [   ]

Paid By : ☐ Cash
          ☐ Check
          ☐ Credit Card

For child care services from : ....
                          To : ....

Balance Due $: ....

Providers EIN Or SSN : ....

Providers Signature :

CHILD CARE RECEIPT

Child's Name : .... Date : ....

Received From : ....

Amount : $ [   ]

Paid By : ☐ Cash
          ☐ Check
          ☐ Credit Card

For child care services from : ....
                          To : ....

Balance Due $: ....

Providers EIN Or SSN : ....

Providers Signature :

CHILD CARE
RECEIPT

Child's Name : .... Date : ....

Received From : .... Amount : $ [   ]

Paid By : ☐ Cash
For child care services from : .... ☐ Check
To : .... ☐ Credit Card

Balance Due $: ....

Providers EIN Or SSN : ....

Providers Signature :

CHILD CARE
RECEIPT

Child's Name : .... Date : ....

Received From : .... Amount : $ [   ]

Paid By : ☐ Cash
For child care services from : .... ☐ Check
To : .... ☐ Credit Card

Balance Due $: ....

Providers EIN Or SSN : ....

Providers Signature :

CHILD CARE
RECEIPT

Child's Name : .... Date : ....

Received From : .... Amount : $ [   ]

Paid By : ☐ Cash
For child care services from : .... ☐ Check
To : .... ☐ Credit Card

Balance Due $: ....

Providers EIN Or SSN : ....

Providers Signature :

CHILD CARE RECEIPT

Child's Name : .... Date : ....

Received From : ....

Amount : $ _____

Paid By : ☐ Cash
☐ Check
☐ Credit Card

For child care services from : ....
To : ....

Balance Due $: ....

Providers EIN Or SSN : ....

Providers Signature :

CHILD CARE RECEIPT

Child's Name : .... Date : ....

Received From : ....

Amount : $ _____

Paid By : ☐ Cash
☐ Check
☐ Credit Card

For child care services from : ....
To : ....

Balance Due $: ....

Providers EIN Or SSN : ....

Providers Signature :

CHILD CARE RECEIPT

Child's Name : .... Date : ....

Received From : ....

Amount : $ _____

Paid By : ☐ Cash
☐ Check
☐ Credit Card

For child care services from : ....
To : ....

Balance Due $: ....

Providers EIN Or SSN : ....

Providers Signature :

CHILD CARE RECEIPT

Child's Name : .... Date : ....

Received From : ....

Amount : $ [   ]

Paid By : ☐ Cash
☐ Check
☐ Credit Card

For child care services from : ....
To : ....
Balance Due $: ....
Providers EIN Or SSN : ....

Providers Signature :

CHILD CARE RECEIPT

Child's Name : .... Date : ....

Received From : ....

Amount : $ [   ]

Paid By : ☐ Cash
☐ Check
☐ Credit Card

For child care services from : ....
To : ....
Balance Due $: ....
Providers EIN Or SSN : ....

Providers Signature :

CHILD CARE RECEIPT

Child's Name : .... Date : ....

Received From : ....

Amount : $ [   ]

Paid By : ☐ Cash
☐ Check
☐ Credit Card

For child care services from : ....
To : ....
Balance Due $: ....
Providers EIN Or SSN : ....

Providers Signature :

CHILD CARE RECEIPT

Child's Name : .... Date : ....

Received From : ....

Amount : $ [   ]

Paid By : ☐ Cash
         ☐ Check
         ☐ Credit Card

For child care services from : ....
                         To : ....

Balance Due $: ....

Providers EIN Or SSN : ....

Providers Signature :

CHILD CARE RECEIPT

Child's Name : .... Date : ....

Received From : ....

Amount : $ [   ]

Paid By : ☐ Cash
         ☐ Check
         ☐ Credit Card

For child care services from : ....
                         To : ....

Balance Due $: ....

Providers EIN Or SSN : ....

Providers Signature :

CHILD CARE RECEIPT

Child's Name : .... Date : ....

Received From : ....

Amount : $ [   ]

Paid By : ☐ Cash
         ☐ Check
         ☐ Credit Card

For child care services from : ....
                         To : ....

Balance Due $: ....

Providers EIN Or SSN : ....

Providers Signature :

CHILD CARE RECEIPT

Child's Name : .... Date : ....

Received From : ....

Amount : $ [   ]

For child care services from : ....

To : ....

Paid By : ☐ Cash
☐ Check
☐ Credit Card

Balance Due $: ....

Providers EIN Or SSN : ....

Providers Signature :

CHILD CARE RECEIPT

Child's Name : .... Date : ....

Received From : ....

Amount : $ [   ]

For child care services from : ....

To : ....

Paid By : ☐ Cash
☐ Check
☐ Credit Card

Balance Due $: ....

Providers EIN Or SSN : ....

Providers Signature :

CHILD CARE RECEIPT

Child's Name : .... Date : ....

Received From : ....

Amount : $ [   ]

For child care services from : ....

To : ....

Paid By : ☐ Cash
☐ Check
☐ Credit Card

Balance Due $: ....

Providers EIN Or SSN : ....

Providers Signature :

CHILD CARE RECEIPT

Child's Name : .... Date : ....

Received From : ....

Amount : $ [   ]

Paid By : ☐ Cash
☐ Check
☐ Credit Card

For child care services from : ....
To : ....
Balance Due $: ....
Providers EIN Or SSN : ....

Providers Signature :

CHILD CARE RECEIPT

Child's Name : .... Date : ....

Received From : ....

Amount : $ [   ]

Paid By : ☐ Cash
☐ Check
☐ Credit Card

For child care services from : ....
To : ....
Balance Due $: ....
Providers EIN Or SSN : ....

Providers Signature :

CHILD CARE RECEIPT

Child's Name : .... Date : ....

Received From : ....

Amount : $ [   ]

Paid By : ☐ Cash
☐ Check
☐ Credit Card

For child care services from : ....
To : ....
Balance Due $: ....
Providers EIN Or SSN : ....

Providers Signature :

CHILD CARE RECEIPT

Child's Name : .... Date : ....

Received From : ....

Amount : $ [   ]

Paid By :
☐ Cash
☐ Check
☐ Credit Card

For child care services from : ....
To : ....
Balance Due $: ....
Providers EIN Or SSN : ....

Providers Signature :

CHILD CARE RECEIPT

Child's Name : .... Date : ....

Received From : ....

Amount : $ [   ]

Paid By :
☐ Cash
☐ Check
☐ Credit Card

For child care services from : ....
To : ....
Balance Due $: ....
Providers EIN Or SSN : ....

Providers Signature :

CHILD CARE RECEIPT

Child's Name : .... Date : ....

Received From : ....

Amount : $ [   ]

Paid By :
☐ Cash
☐ Check
☐ Credit Card

For child care services from : ....
To : ....
Balance Due $: ....
Providers EIN Or SSN : ....

Providers Signature :

CHILD CARE RECEIPT

Child's Name : .... Date : ....

Received From : ....

For child care services from : ....
　　　　　　　　　　To : ....

Balance Due $: ....

Providers EIN Or SSN : ....

Amount : $ [   ]

Paid By : ☐ Cash
　　　　 ☐ Check
　　　　 ☐ Credit Card

Providers Signature :

CHILD CARE RECEIPT

Child's Name : .... Date : ....

Received From : ....

For child care services from : ....
　　　　　　　　　　To : ....

Balance Due $: ....

Providers EIN Or SSN : ....

Amount : $ [   ]

Paid By : ☐ Cash
　　　　 ☐ Check
　　　　 ☐ Credit Card

Providers Signature :

CHILD CARE RECEIPT

Child's Name : .... Date : ....

Received From : ....

For child care services from : ....
　　　　　　　　　　To : ....

Balance Due $: ....

Providers EIN Or SSN : ....

Amount : $ [   ]

Paid By : ☐ Cash
　　　　 ☐ Check
　　　　 ☐ Credit Card

Providers Signature :

CHILD CARE RECEIPT

Child's Name : .... Date : ....

Received From : ....

Amount : $ [   ]

For child care services from : ....
To : ....

Paid By : ☐ Cash
☐ Check
☐ Credit Card

Balance Due $: ....

Providers EIN Or SSN : ....

Providers Signature :

CHILD CARE RECEIPT

Child's Name : .... Date : ....

Received From : ....

Amount : $ [   ]

For child care services from : ....
To : ....

Paid By : ☐ Cash
☐ Check
☐ Credit Card

Balance Due $: ....

Providers EIN Or SSN : ....

Providers Signature :

CHILD CARE RECEIPT

Child's Name : .... Date : ....

Received From : ....

Amount : $ [   ]

For child care services from : ....
To : ....

Paid By : ☐ Cash
☐ Check
☐ Credit Card

Balance Due $: ....

Providers EIN Or SSN : ....

Providers Signature :

CHILD CARE RECEIPT

Child's Name : .... Date : ....

Received From : ....

Amount : $ [   ]

Paid By : ☐ Cash
☐ Check
☐ Credit Card

For child care services from : ....
To : ....
Balance Due $: ....
Providers EIN Or SSN : ....

Providers Signature :

CHILD CARE RECEIPT

Child's Name : .... Date : ....

Received From : ....

Amount : $ [   ]

Paid By : ☐ Cash
☐ Check
☐ Credit Card

For child care services from : ....
To : ....
Balance Due $: ....
Providers EIN Or SSN : ....

Providers Signature :

CHILD CARE RECEIPT

Child's Name : .... Date : ....

Received From : ....

Amount : $ [   ]

Paid By : ☐ Cash
☐ Check
☐ Credit Card

For child care services from : ....
To : ....
Balance Due $: ....
Providers EIN Or SSN : ....

Providers Signature :

CHILD CARE RECEIPT

Child's Name : .... Date : ....

Received From : ....

Amount : $ [   ]

For child care services from : ....
To : ....

Paid By : ☐ Cash
☐ Check
☐ Credit Card

Balance Due $: ....
Providers EIN Or SSN : ....

Providers Signature : _____

CHILD CARE RECEIPT

Child's Name : .... Date : ....

Received From : ....

Amount : $ [   ]

For child care services from : ....
To : ....

Paid By : ☐ Cash
☐ Check
☐ Credit Card

Balance Due $: ....
Providers EIN Or SSN : ....

Providers Signature : _____

CHILD CARE RECEIPT

Child's Name : .... Date : ....

Received From : ....

Amount : $ [   ]

For child care services from : ....
To : ....

Paid By : ☐ Cash
☐ Check
☐ Credit Card

Balance Due $: ....
Providers EIN Or SSN : ....

Providers Signature : _____

CHILD CARE RECEIPT

Child's Name : .... Date : ....

Received From : ....

For child care services from : ....
To : ....

Balance Due $: ....

Providers EIN Or SSN : ....

Amount : $ _____

Paid By : ☐ Cash
☐ Check
☐ Credit Card

Providers Signature :

CHILD CARE RECEIPT

Child's Name : .... Date : ....

Received From : ....

For child care services from : ....
To : ....

Balance Due $: ....
Providers EIN Or SSN : ....

Amount : $ _____

Paid By : ☐ Cash
☐ Check
☐ Credit Card

Providers Signature :

CHILD CARE RECEIPT

Child's Name : .... Date : ....

Received From : ....

For child care services from : ....
To : ....

Balance Due $: ....
Providers EIN Or SSN : ....

Amount : $ _____

Paid By : ☐ Cash
☐ Check
☐ Credit Card

Providers Signature :

CHILD CARE RECEIPT

Child's Name : ....   Date : ....

Received From : ....   Amount : $ [   ]

For child care services from : ....

To : ....

Paid By : ☐ Cash
☐ Check
☐ Credit Card

Balance Due $: ....

Providers EIN Or SSN : ....

Providers Signature :

CHILD CARE RECEIPT

Child's Name : ....   Date : ....

Received From : ....   Amount : $ [   ]

For child care services from : ....

To : ....

Paid By : ☐ Cash
☐ Check
☐ Credit Card

Balance Due $: ....

Providers EIN Or SSN : ....

Providers Signature :

CHILD CARE RECEIPT

Child's Name : ....   Date : ....

Received From : ....   Amount : $ [   ]

For child care services from : ....

To : ....

Paid By : ☐ Cash
☐ Check
☐ Credit Card

Balance Due $: ....

Providers EIN Or SSN : ....

Providers Signature :

CHILD CARE RECEIPT

Child's Name : .... Date : ....

Received From : ....

For child care services from : ....

To : ....

Balance Due $: ....

Providers EIN Or SSN : ....

Amount : $ _____

Paid By : ☐ Cash
☐ Check
☐ Credit Card

Providers Signature :

CHILD CARE RECEIPT

Child's Name : .... Date : ....

Received From : ....

For child care services from : ....

To : ....

Balance Due $: ....

Providers EIN Or SSN : ....

Amount : $ _____

Paid By : ☐ Cash
☐ Check
☐ Credit Card

Providers Signature :

CHILD CARE RECEIPT

Child's Name : .... Date : ....

Received From : ....

For child care services from : ....

To : ....

Balance Due $: ....

Providers EIN Or SSN : ....

Amount : $ _____

Paid By : ☐ Cash
☐ Check
☐ Credit Card

Providers Signature :

CHILD CARE RECEIPT

Child's Name : .... Date : ....

Received From : .... Amount : $ [   ]

For child care services from : ....

To : .... Paid By : ☐ Cash ☐ Check ☐ Credit Card

Balance Due $: ....

Providers EIN Or SSN : ....

Providers Signature :

CHILD CARE RECEIPT

Child's Name : .... Date : ....

Received From : .... Amount : $ [   ]

For child care services from : ....

To : .... Paid By : ☐ Cash ☐ Check ☐ Credit Card

Balance Due $: ....

Providers EIN Or SSN : ....

Providers Signature :

CHILD CARE RECEIPT

Child's Name : .... Date : ....

Received From : .... Amount : $ [   ]

For child care services from : ....

To : .... Paid By : ☐ Cash ☐ Check ☐ Credit Card

Balance Due $: ....

Providers EIN Or SSN : ....

Providers Signature :

CHILD CARE RECEIPT

Child's Name : .... Date : ....

Received From : ....

Amount : $ _____

Paid By : ☐ Cash
         ☐ Check
         ☐ Credit Card

For child care services from : ....
                        To : ....

Balance Due $: ....

Providers EIN Or SSN : ....

Providers Signature :

CHILD CARE RECEIPT

Child's Name : .... Date : ....

Received From : ....

Amount : $ _____

Paid By : ☐ Cash
         ☐ Check
         ☐ Credit Card

For child care services from : ....
                        To : ....

Balance Due $: ....

Providers EIN Or SSN : ....

Providers Signature :

CHILD CARE RECEIPT

Child's Name : .... Date : ....

Received From : ....

Amount : $ _____

Paid By : ☐ Cash
         ☐ Check
         ☐ Credit Card

For child care services from : ....
                        To : ....

Balance Due $: ....

Providers EIN Or SSN : ....

Providers Signature :

CHILD CARE RECEIPT

Child's Name : .... Date : ....

Received From : ....

Amount : $ [   ]

Paid By : ☐ Cash
☐ Check
☐ Credit Card

For child care services from : ....
To : ....

Balance Due $: ....
Providers EIN Or SSN : ....

Providers Signature :

CHILD CARE RECEIPT

Child's Name : .... Date : ....

Received From : ....

Amount : $ [   ]

Paid By : ☐ Cash
☐ Check
☐ Credit Card

For child care services from : ....
To : ....

Balance Due $: ....
Providers EIN Or SSN : ....

Providers Signature :

CHILD CARE RECEIPT

Child's Name : .... Date : ....

Received From : ....

Amount : $ [   ]

Paid By : ☐ Cash
☐ Check
☐ Credit Card

For child care services from : ....
To : ....

Balance Due $: ....
Providers EIN Or SSN : ....

Providers Signature :

CHILD CARE RECEIPT

Child's Name : ....   Date : ....

Received From : ....

Amount : $ [   ]

Paid By : ☐ Cash
           ☐ Check
           ☐ Credit Card

For child care services from : ....
                        To : ....

Balance Due $: ....

Providers EIN Or SSN : ....

Providers Signature : ....

CHILD CARE RECEIPT

Child's Name : ....   Date : ....

Received From : ....

Amount : $ [   ]

Paid By : ☐ Cash
           ☐ Check
           ☐ Credit Card

For child care services from : ....
                        To : ....

Balance Due $: ....

Providers EIN Or SSN : ....

Providers Signature : ....

CHILD CARE RECEIPT

Child's Name : ....   Date : ....

Received From : ....

Amount : $ [   ]

Paid By : ☐ Cash
           ☐ Check
           ☐ Credit Card

For child care services from : ....
                        To : ....

Balance Due $: ....

Providers EIN Or SSN : ....

Providers Signature : ....

CHILD CARE RECEIPT

Child's Name : .... Date : ....

Received From : ....

For child care services from : ....
                        To : ....

Balance Due $: ....

Providers EIN Or SSN : ....

Amount : $ [_____]

Paid By : ☐ Cash
         ☐ Check
         ☐ Credit Card

Providers Signature :

CHILD CARE RECEIPT

Child's Name : .... Date : ....

Received From : ....

For child care services from : ....
                        To : ....

Balance Due $: ....

Providers EIN Or SSN : ....

Amount : $ [_____]

Paid By : ☐ Cash
         ☐ Check
         ☐ Credit Card

Providers Signature :

CHILD CARE RECEIPT

Child's Name : .... Date : ....

Received From : ....

For child care services from : ....
                        To : ....

Balance Due $: ....

Providers EIN Or SSN : ....

Amount : $ [_____]

Paid By : ☐ Cash
         ☐ Check
         ☐ Credit Card

Providers Signature :

CHILD CARE RECEIPT

Child's Name : ....   Date : ....

Received From : ....   Amount : $ [   ]

Paid By : ☐ Cash
For child care services from : ....   ☐ Check
                        To : ....   ☐ Credit Card

Balance Due $: ....

Providers EIN Or SSN : ....

Providers Signature :

CHILD CARE RECEIPT

Child's Name : ....   Date : ....

Received From : ....   Amount : $ [   ]

Paid By : ☐ Cash
For child care services from : ....   ☐ Check
                        To : ....   ☐ Credit Card

Balance Due $: ....

Providers EIN Or SSN : ....

Providers Signature :

CHILD CARE RECEIPT

Child's Name : ....   Date : ....

Received From : ....   Amount : $ [   ]

Paid By : ☐ Cash
For child care services from : ....   ☐ Check
                        To : ....   ☐ Credit Card

Balance Due $: ....

Providers EIN Or SSN : ....

Providers Signature :

CHILD CARE RECEIPT

Child's Name : .... Date : ....

Received From : .... Amount : $ _____

Paid By : ☐ Cash
☐ Check
☐ Credit Card

For child care services from : ....
To : ....

Balance Due $: ....

Providers EIN Or SSN : ....

Providers Signature :

CHILD CARE RECEIPT

Child's Name : .... Date : ....

Received From : .... Amount : $ _____

Paid By : ☐ Cash
☐ Check
☐ Credit Card

For child care services from : ....
To : ....

Balance Due $: ....

Providers EIN Or SSN : ....

Providers Signature :

CHILD CARE RECEIPT

Child's Name : .... Date : ....

Received From : .... Amount : $ _____

Paid By : ☐ Cash
☐ Check
☐ Credit Card

For child care services from : ....
To : ....

Balance Due $: ....

Providers EIN Or SSN : ....

Providers Signature :

CHILD CARE RECEIPT

Child's Name : .... Date : ....

Received From : ....

Amount : $ [   ]

Paid By : ☐ Cash
           ☐ Check
           ☐ Credit Card

For child care services from : ....
                          To : ....

Balance Due $: ....

Providers EIN Or SSN : ....

Providers Signature :

CHILD CARE RECEIPT

Child's Name : .... Date : ....

Received From : ....

Amount : $ [   ]

Paid By : ☐ Cash
           ☐ Check
           ☐ Credit Card

For child care services from : ....
                          To : ....

Balance Due $: ....

Providers EIN Or SSN : ....

Providers Signature :

CHILD CARE RECEIPT

Child's Name : .... Date : ....

Received From : ....

Amount : $ [   ]

Paid By : ☐ Cash
           ☐ Check
           ☐ Credit Card

For child care services from : ....
                          To : ....

Balance Due $: ....

Providers EIN Or SSN : ....

Providers Signature :

CHILD CARE RECEIPT

Child's Name : .... Date : ....

Received From : ....

Amount : $[   ]

For child care services from : ....
To : ....

Paid By : ☐ Cash
☐ Check
☐ Credit Card

Balance Due $: ....

Providers EIN Or SSN : ....

Providers Signature :

CHILD CARE RECEIPT

Child's Name : .... Date : ....

Received From : ....

Amount : $[   ]

For child care services from : ....
To : ....

Paid By : ☐ Cash
☐ Check
☐ Credit Card

Balance Due $: ....

Providers EIN Or SSN : ....

Providers Signature :

CHILD CARE RECEIPT

Child's Name : .... Date : ....

Received From : ....

Amount : $[   ]

For child care services from : ....
To : ....

Paid By : ☐ Cash
☐ Check
☐ Credit Card

Balance Due $: ....

Providers EIN Or SSN : ....

Providers Signature :

CHILD CARE
RECEIPT

Child's Name : .... Date : ....

Received From : ....   Amount : $ [   ]

For child care services from : ....   Paid By : ☐ Cash
To : ....   ☐ Check
Balance Due $: ....   ☐ Credit Card
Providers EIN Or SSN : ....

Providers Signature :

CHILD CARE
RECEIPT

Child's Name : .... Date : ....

Received From : ....   Amount : $ [   ]

For child care services from : ....   Paid By : ☐ Cash
To : ....   ☐ Check
Balance Due $: ....   ☐ Credit Card
Providers EIN Or SSN : ....

Providers Signature :

CHILD CARE
RECEIPT

Child's Name : .... Date : ....

Received From : ....   Amount : $ [   ]

For child care services from : ....   Paid By : ☐ Cash
To : ....   ☐ Check
Balance Due $: ....   ☐ Credit Card
Providers EIN Or SSN : ....

Providers Signature :

CHILD CARE RECEIPT

Child's Name : .... Date : ....

Received From : ....

Amount : $ [   ]

Paid By : ☐ Cash
☐ Check
☐ Credit Card

For child care services from : ....
To : ....

Balance Due $: ....

Providers EIN Or SSN : ....

Providers Signature :

CHILD CARE RECEIPT

Child's Name : .... Date : ....

Received From : ....

Amount : $ [   ]

Paid By : ☐ Cash
☐ Check
☐ Credit Card

For child care services from : ....
To : ....

Balance Due $: ....

Providers EIN Or SSN : ....

Providers Signature :

CHILD CARE RECEIPT

Child's Name : .... Date : ....

Received From : ....

Amount : $ [   ]

Paid By : ☐ Cash
☐ Check
☐ Credit Card

For child care services from : ....
To : ....

Balance Due $: ....

Providers EIN Or SSN : ....

Providers Signature :

CHILD CARE RECEIPT

Child's Name : ....   Date : ....

Received From : ....

For child care services from : ....
To : ....

Balance Due $: ....

Providers EIN Or SSN : ....

Providers Signature :

Amount : $ _____

Paid By : ☐ Cash
☐ Check
☐ Credit Card

CHILD CARE RECEIPT

Child's Name : ....   Date : ....

Received From : ....

For child care services from : ....
To : ....

Balance Due $: ....

Providers EIN Or SSN : ....

Providers Signature :

Amount : $ _____

Paid By : ☐ Cash
☐ Check
☐ Credit Card

CHILD CARE RECEIPT

Child's Name : ....   Date : ....

Received From : ....

For child care services from : ....
To : ....

Balance Due $: ....

Providers EIN Or SSN : ....

Providers Signature :

Amount : $ _____

Paid By : ☐ Cash
☐ Check
☐ Credit Card

CHILD CARE
RECEIPT

Child's Name : .... Date : ....

Received From : ....

Amount : $ [   ]

Paid By : ☐ Cash
☐ Check
☐ Credit Card

For child care services from : ....
To : ....
Balance Due $: ....
Providers EIN Or SSN : ....

Providers Signature :

CHILD CARE
RECEIPT

Child's Name : .... Date : ....

Received From : ....

Amount : $ [   ]

Paid By : ☐ Cash
☐ Check
☐ Credit Card

For child care services from : ....
To : ....
Balance Due $: ....
Providers EIN Or SSN : ....

Providers Signature :

CHILD CARE
RECEIPT

Child's Name : .... Date : ....

Received From : ....

Amount : $ [   ]

Paid By : ☐ Cash
☐ Check
☐ Credit Card

For child care services from : ....
To : ....
Balance Due $: ....
Providers EIN Or SSN : ....

Providers Signature :

CHILD CARE RECEIPT

Child's Name : ....   Date : ....

Received From : ....

For child care services from : ....
                        To : ....

Balance Due $: ....

Providers EIN Or SSN : ....

Amount : $ [   ]

Paid By : ☐ Cash
         ☐ Check
         ☐ Credit Card

Providers Signature :

CHILD CARE RECEIPT

Child's Name : ....   Date : ....

Received From : ....

For child care services from : ....
                        To : ....

Balance Due $: ....

Providers EIN Or SSN : ....

Amount : $ [   ]

Paid By : ☐ Cash
         ☐ Check
         ☐ Credit Card

Providers Signature :

CHILD CARE RECEIPT

Child's Name : ....   Date : ....

Received From : ....

For child care services from : ....
                        To : ....

Balance Due $: ....

Providers EIN Or SSN : ....

Amount : $ [   ]

Paid By : ☐ Cash
         ☐ Check
         ☐ Credit Card

Providers Signature :

CHILD CARE RECEIPT

Child's Name : .... Date : ....

Received From : .... Amount : $ [ ]

For child care services from : ....

To : ....

Balance Due $: ....

Providers EIN Or SSN : ....

Paid By : ☐ Cash
☐ Check
☐ Credit Card

Providers Signature :

CHILD CARE RECEIPT

Child's Name : .... Date : ....

Received From : .... Amount : $ [ ]

For child care services from : ....

To : ....

Balance Due $: ....

Providers EIN Or SSN : ....

Paid By : ☐ Cash
☐ Check
☐ Credit Card

Providers Signature :

CHILD CARE RECEIPT

Child's Name : .... Date : ....

Received From : .... Amount : $ [ ]

For child care services from : ....

To : ....

Balance Due $: ....

Providers EIN Or SSN : ....

Paid By : ☐ Cash
☐ Check
☐ Credit Card

Providers Signature :

CHILD CARE RECEIPT

Child's Name : .... Date : ....

Received From : .... Amount : $ [   ]

Paid By : ☐ Cash
☐ Check
☐ Credit Card

For child care services from : ....
To : ....
Balance Due $: ....
Providers EIN Or SSN : ....

Providers Signature :

CHILD CARE RECEIPT

Child's Name : .... Date : ....

Received From : .... Amount : $ [   ]

Paid By : ☐ Cash
☐ Check
☐ Credit Card

For child care services from : ....
To : ....
Balance Due $: ....
Providers EIN Or SSN : ....

Providers Signature :

CHILD CARE RECEIPT

Child's Name : .... Date : ....

Received From : .... Amount : $ [   ]

Paid By : ☐ Cash
☐ Check
☐ Credit Card

For child care services from : ....
To : ....
Balance Due $: ....
Providers EIN Or SSN : ....

Providers Signature :

CHILD CARE RECEIPT

Child's Name : ....   Date : ....

Received From : ....   Amount : $ [   ]

Paid By : ☐ Cash
          ☐ Check
          ☐ Credit Card

For child care services from : ....

To : ....

Balance Due $: ....

Providers EIN Or SSN : ....

Providers Signature :

CHILD CARE RECEIPT

Child's Name : ....   Date : ....

Received From : ....   Amount : $ [   ]

Paid By : ☐ Cash
          ☐ Check
          ☐ Credit Card

For child care services from : ....

To : ....

Balance Due $: ....

Providers EIN Or SSN : ....

Providers Signature :

CHILD CARE RECEIPT

Child's Name : ....   Date : ....

Received From : ....   Amount : $ [   ]

Paid By : ☐ Cash
          ☐ Check
          ☐ Credit Card

For child care services from : ....

To : ....

Balance Due $: ....

Providers EIN Or SSN : ....

Providers Signature :

CHILD CARE RECEIPT

Child's Name : .... Date : ....

Received From : ....

Amount : $ [   ]

Paid By : ☐ Cash
☐ Check
☐ Credit Card

For child care services from : ....
To : ....

Balance Due $: ....

Providers EIN Or SSN : ....

Providers Signature : ....

CHILD CARE RECEIPT

Child's Name : .... Date : ....

Received From : ....

Amount : $ [   ]

Paid By : ☐ Cash
☐ Check
☐ Credit Card

For child care services from : ....
To : ....

Balance Due $: ....

Providers EIN Or SSN : ....

Providers Signature : ....

CHILD CARE RECEIPT

Child's Name : .... Date : ....

Received From : ....

Amount : $ [   ]

Paid By : ☐ Cash
☐ Check
☐ Credit Card

For child care services from : ....
To : ....

Balance Due $: ....

Providers EIN Or SSN : ....

Providers Signature : ....

CHILD CARE RECEIPT

Child's Name : .... Date : ....

Received From : ....

Amount : $ [   ]

Paid By : ☐ Cash
           ☐ Check
           ☐ Credit Card

For child care services from : ....
                          To : ....
Balance Due $: ....
Providers EIN Or SSN : ....

Providers Signature : ....

CHILD CARE RECEIPT

Child's Name : .... Date : ....

Received From : ....

Amount : $ [   ]

Paid By : ☐ Cash
           ☐ Check
           ☐ Credit Card

For child care services from : ....
                          To : ....
Balance Due $: ....
Providers EIN Or SSN : ....

Providers Signature : ....

CHILD CARE RECEIPT

Child's Name : .... Date : ....

Received From : ....

Amount : $ [   ]

Paid By : ☐ Cash
           ☐ Check
           ☐ Credit Card

For child care services from : ....
                          To : ....
Balance Due $: ....
Providers EIN Or SSN : ....

Providers Signature : ....

CHILD CARE RECEIPT

Child's Name : ....   Date : ....

Received From : ....   Amount : $ [   ]

For child care services from : ....

To : ....   Paid By : ☐ Cash
                                                 ☐ Check
                                                 ☐ Credit Card

Balance Due $: ....

Providers EIN Or SSN : ....

Providers Signature :

CHILD CARE RECEIPT

Child's Name : ....   Date : ....

Received From : ....   Amount : $ [   ]

For child care services from : ....

To : ....   Paid By : ☐ Cash
                                                 ☐ Check
                                                 ☐ Credit Card

Balance Due $: ....

Providers EIN Or SSN : ....

Providers Signature :

CHILD CARE RECEIPT

Child's Name : ....   Date : ....

Received From : ....   Amount : $ [   ]

For child care services from : ....

To : ....   Paid By : ☐ Cash
                                                 ☐ Check
                                                 ☐ Credit Card

Balance Due $: ....

Providers EIN Or SSN : ....

Providers Signature :

CHILD CARE RECEIPT

Child's Name : .... Date : ....

Received From : .... Amount : $ [   ]

For child care services from : .... Paid By : ☐ Cash
            To : .... ☐ Check
Balance Due $: .... ☐ Credit Card
Providers EIN Or SSN : ....
            Providers Signature :

CHILD CARE RECEIPT

Child's Name : .... Date : ....

Received From : .... Amount : $ [   ]

For child care services from : .... Paid By : ☐ Cash
            To : .... ☐ Check
Balance Due $: .... ☐ Credit Card
Providers EIN Or SSN : ....
            Providers Signature :

CHILD CARE RECEIPT

Child's Name : .... Date : ....

Received From : .... Amount : $ [   ]

For child care services from : .... Paid By : ☐ Cash
            To : .... ☐ Check
Balance Due $: .... ☐ Credit Card
Providers EIN Or SSN : ....
            Providers Signature :

CHILD CARE RECEIPT

Child's Name : .... Date : ....

Received From : ....

For child care services from : ....
To : ....

Balance Due $: ....

Providers EIN Or SSN : ....

Amount : $ [   ]

Paid By : ☐ Cash
☐ Check
☐ Credit Card

Providers Signature :

CHILD CARE RECEIPT

Child's Name : .... Date : ....

Received From : ....

For child care services from : ....
To : ....

Balance Due $: ....

Providers EIN Or SSN : ....

Amount : $ [   ]

Paid By : ☐ Cash
☐ Check
☐ Credit Card

Providers Signature :

CHILD CARE RECEIPT

Child's Name : .... Date : ....

Received From : ....

For child care services from : ....
To : ....

Balance Due $: ....

Providers EIN Or SSN : ....

Amount : $ [   ]

Paid By : ☐ Cash
☐ Check
☐ Credit Card

Providers Signature :

CHILD CARE RECEIPT

Child's Name : .... Date : ....

Received From : ....

Amount : $ [   ]

Paid By : ☐ Cash
☐ Check
☐ Credit Card

For child care services from : ....
To : ....

Balance Due $: ....

Providers EIN Or SSN : ....

Providers Signature :

CHILD CARE RECEIPT

Child's Name : .... Date : ....

Received From : ....

Amount : $ [   ]

Paid By : ☐ Cash
☐ Check
☐ Credit Card

For child care services from : ....
To : ....

Balance Due $: ....

Providers EIN Or SSN : ....

Providers Signature :

CHILD CARE RECEIPT

Child's Name : .... Date : ....

Received From : ....

Amount : $ [   ]

Paid By : ☐ Cash
☐ Check
☐ Credit Card

For child care services from : ....
To : ....

Balance Due $: ....

Providers EIN Or SSN : ....

Providers Signature :

CHILD CARE RECEIPT

Child's Name : ....   Date : ....

Received From : ....   Amount : $ _____

For child care services from : ....   Paid By : ☐ Cash
                           To : ....   ☐ Check

Balance Due $: ....   ☐ Credit Card

Providers EIN Or SSN : ....

                     Providers Signature : _____

CHILD CARE RECEIPT

Child's Name : ....   Date : ....

Received From : ....   Amount : $ _____

For child care services from : ....   Paid By : ☐ Cash
                           To : ....   ☐ Check

Balance Due $: ....   ☐ Credit Card

Providers EIN Or SSN : ....

                     Providers Signature : _____

CHILD CARE RECEIPT

Child's Name : ....   Date : ....

Received From : ....   Amount : $ _____

For child care services from : ....   Paid By : ☐ Cash
                           To : ....   ☐ Check

Balance Due $: ....   ☐ Credit Card

Providers EIN Or SSN : ....

                     Providers Signature : _____

CHILD CARE RECEIPT

Child's Name : ....   Date : ....

Received From : ....

Amount : $ [ ]

Paid By : ☐ Cash
            ☐ Check
            ☐ Credit Card

For child care services from : ....
                   To : ....

Balance Due $: ....

Providers EIN Or SSN : ....

Providers Signature :

CHILD CARE RECEIPT

Child's Name : ....   Date : ....

Received From : ....

Amount : $ [ ]

Paid By : ☐ Cash
            ☐ Check
            ☐ Credit Card

For child care services from : ....
                   To : ....

Balance Due $: ....

Providers EIN Or SSN : ....

Providers Signature :

CHILD CARE RECEIPT

Child's Name : ....   Date : ....

Received From : ....

Amount : $ [ ]

Paid By : ☐ Cash
            ☐ Check
            ☐ Credit Card

For child care services from : ....
                   To : ....

Balance Due $: ....

Providers EIN Or SSN : ....

Providers Signature :

CHILD CARE
RECEIPT

Child's Name : .... Date : ....

Received From : ....

Amount : $ [   ]

Paid By : ☐ Cash
☐ Check
☐ Credit Card

For child care services from : ....
To : ....

Balance Due $: ....

Providers EIN Or SSN : ....

Providers Signature :

CHILD CARE
RECEIPT

Child's Name : .... Date : ....

Received From : ....

Amount : $ [   ]

Paid By : ☐ Cash
☐ Check
☐ Credit Card

For child care services from : ....
To : ....

Balance Due $: ....

Providers EIN Or SSN : ....

Providers Signature :

CHILD CARE
RECEIPT

Child's Name : .... Date : ....

Received From : ....

Amount : $ [   ]

Paid By : ☐ Cash
☐ Check
☐ Credit Card

For child care services from : ....
To : ....

Balance Due $: ....

Providers EIN Or SSN : ....

Providers Signature :

CHILD CARE RECEIPT

Child's Name : .... Date : ....

Received From : .... Amount : $ _____

Paid By : ☐ Cash
☐ Check
For child care services from : .... ☐ Credit Card
To : ....
Balance Due $: ....
Providers EIN Or SSN : ....
Providers Signature : ....

CHILD CARE RECEIPT

Child's Name : .... Date : ....

Received From : .... Amount : $ _____

Paid By : ☐ Cash
☐ Check
For child care services from : .... ☐ Credit Card
To : ....
Balance Due $: ....
Providers EIN Or SSN : ....
Providers Signature : ....

CHILD CARE RECEIPT

Child's Name : .... Date : ....

Received From : .... Amount : $ _____

Paid By : ☐ Cash
☐ Check
For child care services from : .... ☐ Credit Card
To : ....
Balance Due $: ....
Providers EIN Or SSN : ....
Providers Signature : ....

CHILD CARE RECEIPT

Child's Name : .... Date : ....

Received From : ....

Amount : $ [   ]

Paid By : ☐ Cash
☐ Check
☐ Credit Card

For child care services from : ....
To : ....

Balance Due $: ....

Providers EIN Or SSN : ....

Providers Signature : ....

CHILD CARE RECEIPT

Child's Name : .... Date : ....

Received From : ....

Amount : $ [   ]

Paid By : ☐ Cash
☐ Check
☐ Credit Card

For child care services from : ....
To : ....

Balance Due $: ....

Providers EIN Or SSN : ....

Providers Signature : ....

CHILD CARE RECEIPT

Child's Name : .... Date : ....

Received From : ....

Amount : $ [   ]

Paid By : ☐ Cash
☐ Check
☐ Credit Card

For child care services from : ....
To : ....

Balance Due $: ....

Providers EIN Or SSN : ....

Providers Signature : ....

CHILD CARE RECEIPT

Child's Name : .... Date : ....

Received From : .... Amount : $ [   ]

Paid By : ☐ Cash
           ☐ Check
           ☐ Credit Card

For child care services from : ....
                         To : ....
Balance Due $: ....
Providers EIN Or SSN : ....

Providers Signature :

CHILD CARE RECEIPT

Child's Name : .... Date : ....

Received From : .... Amount : $ [   ]

Paid By : ☐ Cash
           ☐ Check
           ☐ Credit Card

For child care services from : ....
                         To : ....
Balance Due $: ....
Providers EIN Or SSN : ....

Providers Signature :

CHILD CARE RECEIPT

Child's Name : .... Date : ....

Received From : .... Amount : $ [   ]

Paid By : ☐ Cash
           ☐ Check
           ☐ Credit Card

For child care services from : ....
                         To : ....
Balance Due $: ....
Providers EIN Or SSN : ....

Providers Signature :

CHILD CARE RECEIPT

Child's Name : .... Date : ....

Received From : ....

Amount : $ [   ]

Paid By : ☐ Cash
☐ Check
☐ Credit Card

For child care services from : ....
To : ....

Balance Due $: ....

Providers EIN Or SSN : ....

Providers Signature :

CHILD CARE RECEIPT

Child's Name : .... Date : ....

Received From : ....

Amount : $ [   ]

Paid By : ☐ Cash
☐ Check
☐ Credit Card

For child care services from : ....
To : ....

Balance Due $: ....

Providers EIN Or SSN : ....

Providers Signature :

CHILD CARE RECEIPT

Child's Name : .... Date : ....

Received From : ....

Amount : $ [   ]

Paid By : ☐ Cash
☐ Check
☐ Credit Card

For child care services from : ....
To : ....

Balance Due $: ....

Providers EIN Or SSN : ....

Providers Signature :

CHILD CARE RECEIPT

Child's Name : .... Date : ....

Received From : ....

Amount : $ _____

Paid By : ☐ Cash
☐ Check
☐ Credit Card

For child care services from : ....
To : ....

Balance Due $: ....

Providers EIN Or SSN : ....

Providers Signature :

CHILD CARE RECEIPT

Child's Name : .... Date : ....

Received From : ....

Amount : $ _____

Paid By : ☐ Cash
☐ Check
☐ Credit Card

For child care services from : ....
To : ....

Balance Due $: ....

Providers EIN Or SSN : ....

Providers Signature :

CHILD CARE RECEIPT

Child's Name : .... Date : ....

Received From : ....

Amount : $ _____

Paid By : ☐ Cash
☐ Check
☐ Credit Card

For child care services from : ....
To : ....

Balance Due $: ....

Providers EIN Or SSN : ....

Providers Signature :

CHILD CARE RECEIPT

Child's Name : .... Date : ....

Received From : ....

Amount : $ _____

For child care services from : ....

To : ....

Paid By : ☐ Cash
☐ Check
☐ Credit Card

Balance Due $: ....

Providers EIN Or SSN : ....

Providers Signature :

CHILD CARE RECEIPT

Child's Name : .... Date : ....

Received From : ....

Amount : $ _____

For child care services from : ....

To : ....

Paid By : ☐ Cash
☐ Check
☐ Credit Card

Balance Due $: ....

Providers EIN Or SSN : ....

Providers Signature :

CHILD CARE RECEIPT

Child's Name : .... Date : ....

Received From : ....

Amount : $ _____

For child care services from : ....

To : ....

Paid By : ☐ Cash
☐ Check
☐ Credit Card

Balance Due $: ....

Providers EIN Or SSN : ....

Providers Signature :

CHILD CARE RECEIPT

Child's Name : .... Date : ....

Received From : .... Amount : $ [   ]

Paid By : ☐ Cash
            ☐ Check
For child care services from : .... ☐ Credit Card
           To : ....

Balance Due $: ....

Providers EIN Or SSN : ....

Providers Signature :

CHILD CARE RECEIPT

Child's Name : .... Date : ....

Received From : .... Amount : $ [   ]

Paid By : ☐ Cash
            ☐ Check
For child care services from : .... ☐ Credit Card
           To : ....

Balance Due $: ....

Providers EIN Or SSN : ....

Providers Signature :

CHILD CARE RECEIPT

Child's Name : .... Date : ....

Received From : .... Amount : $ [   ]

Paid By : ☐ Cash
            ☐ Check
For child care services from : .... ☐ Credit Card
           To : ....

Balance Due $: ....

Providers EIN Or SSN : ....

Providers Signature :

CHILD CARE RECEIPT

Child's Name : .... Date : ....

Received From : ....

Amount : $ [   ]

Paid By : ☐ Cash
          ☐ Check
          ☐ Credit Card

For child care services from : ....
To : ....

Balance Due $: ....

Providers EIN Or SSN : ....

Providers Signature :

CHILD CARE RECEIPT

Child's Name : .... Date : ....

Received From : ....

Amount : $ [   ]

Paid By : ☐ Cash
          ☐ Check
          ☐ Credit Card

For child care services from : ....
To : ....

Balance Due $: ....

Providers EIN Or SSN : ....

Providers Signature :

CHILD CARE RECEIPT

Child's Name : .... Date : ....

Received From : ....

Amount : $ [   ]

Paid By : ☐ Cash
          ☐ Check
          ☐ Credit Card

For child care services from : ....
To : ....

Balance Due $: ....

Providers EIN Or SSN : ....

Providers Signature :

CHILD CARE RECEIPT

Child's Name : .... Date : ....

Received From : ....

Amount : $ [   ]

Paid By : ☐ Cash
☐ Check
☐ Credit Card

For child care services from : ....
To : ....

Balance Due $: ....

Providers EIN Or SSN : ....

Providers Signature :

CHILD CARE RECEIPT

Child's Name : .... Date : ....

Received From : ....

Amount : $ [   ]

Paid By : ☐ Cash
☐ Check
☐ Credit Card

For child care services from : ....
To : ....

Balance Due $: ....

Providers EIN Or SSN : ....

Providers Signature :

CHILD CARE RECEIPT

Child's Name : .... Date : ....

Received From : ....

Amount : $ [   ]

Paid By : ☐ Cash
☐ Check
☐ Credit Card

For child care services from : ....
To : ....

Balance Due $: ....

Providers EIN Or SSN : ....

Providers Signature :

CHILD CARE RECEIPT

Child's Name : .... Date : ....

Received From : .... Amount : $ _____

Paid By : ☐ Cash
☐ Check
☐ Credit Card

For child care services from : ....
To : ....

Balance Due $: ....

Providers EIN Or SSN : ....

Providers Signature : _____

CHILD CARE RECEIPT

Child's Name : .... Date : ....

Received From : .... Amount : $ _____

Paid By : ☐ Cash
☐ Check
☐ Credit Card

For child care services from : ....
To : ....

Balance Due $: ....

Providers EIN Or SSN : ....

Providers Signature : _____

CHILD CARE RECEIPT

Child's Name : .... Date : ....

Received From : .... Amount : $ _____

Paid By : ☐ Cash
☐ Check
☐ Credit Card

For child care services from : ....
To : ....

Balance Due $: ....

Providers EIN Or SSN : ....

Providers Signature : _____

CHILD CARE RECEIPT

Child's Name : .... Date : ....

Received From : .... Amount : $ [   ]

Paid By : ☐ Cash
For child care services from : .... ☐ Check
To : .... ☐ Credit Card
Balance Due $: ....
Providers EIN Or SSN : ....
Providers Signature :

CHILD CARE RECEIPT

Child's Name : .... Date : ....

Received From : .... Amount : $ [   ]

Paid By : ☐ Cash
For child care services from : .... ☐ Check
To : .... ☐ Credit Card
Balance Due $: ....
Providers EIN Or SSN : ....
Providers Signature :

CHILD CARE RECEIPT

Child's Name : .... Date : ....

Received From : .... Amount : $ [   ]

Paid By : ☐ Cash
For child care services from : .... ☐ Check
To : .... ☐ Credit Card
Balance Due $: ....
Providers EIN Or SSN : ....
Providers Signature :

CHILD CARE
RECEIPT

Child's Name : .... Date : ....

Received From : ....

Amount : $ [   ]

Paid By : ☐ Cash
         ☐ Check
         ☐ Credit Card

For child care services from : ....
                          To : ....

Balance Due $: ....

Providers EIN Or SSN : ....

Providers Signature :

CHILD CARE
RECEIPT

Child's Name : .... Date : ....

Received From : ....

Amount : $ [   ]

Paid By : ☐ Cash
         ☐ Check
         ☐ Credit Card

For child care services from : ....
                          To : ....

Balance Due $: ....

Providers EIN Or SSN : ....

Providers Signature :

CHILD CARE
RECEIPT

Child's Name : .... Date : ....

Received From : ....

Amount : $ [   ]

Paid By : ☐ Cash
         ☐ Check
         ☐ Credit Card

For child care services from : ....
                          To : ....

Balance Due $: ....

Providers EIN Or SSN : ....

Providers Signature :

CHILD CARE RECEIPT

Child's Name : ....   Date : ....

Received From : ....

Amount : $

Paid By : ☐ Cash
☐ Check
☐ Credit Card

For child care services from : ....
To : ....

Balance Due $: ....

Providers EIN Or SSN : ....

Providers Signature :

CHILD CARE RECEIPT

Child's Name : ....   Date : ....

Received From : ....

Amount : $

Paid By : ☐ Cash
☐ Check
☐ Credit Card

For child care services from : ....
To : ....

Balance Due $: ....

Providers EIN Or SSN : ....

Providers Signature :

CHILD CARE RECEIPT

Child's Name : ....   Date : ....

Received From : ....

Amount : $

Paid By : ☐ Cash
☐ Check
☐ Credit Card

For child care services from : ....
To : ....

Balance Due $: ....

Providers EIN Or SSN : ....

Providers Signature :

CHILD CARE RECEIPT

Child's Name : ....   Date : ....

Received From : ....   Amount : $ [   ]

For child care services from : ....
                        To : ....

Paid By : ☐ Cash
           ☐ Check
           ☐ Credit Card

Balance Due $: ....

Providers EIN Or SSN : ....

Providers Signature :

CHILD CARE RECEIPT

Child's Name : ....   Date : ....

Received From : ....   Amount : $ [   ]

For child care services from : ....
                        To : ....

Paid By : ☐ Cash
           ☐ Check
           ☐ Credit Card

Balance Due $: ....

Providers EIN Or SSN : ....

Providers Signature :

CHILD CARE RECEIPT

Child's Name : ....   Date : ....

Received From : ....   Amount : $ [   ]

For child care services from : ....
                        To : ....

Paid By : ☐ Cash
           ☐ Check
           ☐ Credit Card

Balance Due $: ....

Providers EIN Or SSN : ....

Providers Signature :

CHILD CARE RECEIPT

Child's Name : .... Date : ....

Received From : ....

Amount : $ [   ]

Paid By : ☐ Cash
☐ Check
☐ Credit Card

For child care services from : ....
To : ....

Balance Due $: ....

Providers EIN Or SSN : ....

Providers Signature :

CHILD CARE RECEIPT

Child's Name : .... Date : ....

Received From : ....

Amount : $ [   ]

Paid By : ☐ Cash
☐ Check
☐ Credit Card

For child care services from : ....
To : ....

Balance Due $: ....

Providers EIN Or SSN : ....

Providers Signature :

CHILD CARE RECEIPT

Child's Name : .... Date : ....

Received From : ....

Amount : $ [   ]

Paid By : ☐ Cash
☐ Check
☐ Credit Card

For child care services from : ....
To : ....

Balance Due $: ....

Providers EIN Or SSN : ....

Providers Signature :

CHILD CARE
RECEIPT

Child's Name : .... Date : ....

Received From : ....

Amount : $ [____]

Paid By : ☐ Cash
          ☐ Check
          ☐ Credit Card

For child care services from : ....
                          To : ....

Balance Due $: ....

Providers EIN Or SSN : ....

Providers Signature :

CHILD CARE
RECEIPT

Child's Name : .... Date : ....

Received From : ....

Amount : $ [____]

Paid By : ☐ Cash
          ☐ Check
          ☐ Credit Card

For child care services from : ....
                          To : ....

Balance Due $: ....

Providers EIN Or SSN : ....

Providers Signature :

CHILD CARE
RECEIPT

Child's Name : .... Date : ....

Received From : ....

Amount : $ [____]

Paid By : ☐ Cash
          ☐ Check
          ☐ Credit Card

For child care services from : ....
                          To : ....

Balance Due $: ....

Providers EIN Or SSN : ....

Providers Signature :

CHILD CARE RECEIPT

Child's Name : .... Date : ....

Received From : .... Amount : $ [   ]

For child care services from : .... Paid By : ☐ Cash
                        To : .... ☐ Check
Balance Due $: .... ☐ Credit Card
Providers EIN Or SSN : ....
                        Providers Signature :

CHILD CARE RECEIPT

Child's Name : .... Date : ....

Received From : .... Amount : $ [   ]

For child care services from : .... Paid By : ☐ Cash
                        To : .... ☐ Check
Balance Due $: .... ☐ Credit Card
Providers EIN Or SSN : ....
                        Providers Signature :

CHILD CARE RECEIPT

Child's Name : .... Date : ....

Received From : .... Amount : $ [   ]

For child care services from : .... Paid By : ☐ Cash
                        To : .... ☐ Check
Balance Due $: .... ☐ Credit Card
Providers EIN Or SSN : ....
                        Providers Signature :

CHILD CARE RECEIPT

Child's Name : .... Date : ....

Received From : ....

Amount : $ [   ]

Paid By : ☐ Cash
☐ Check
☐ Credit Card

For child care services from : ....
To : ....

Balance Due $: ....

Providers EIN Or SSN : ....

Providers Signature :

CHILD CARE RECEIPT

Child's Name : .... Date : ....

Received From : ....

Amount : $ [   ]

Paid By : ☐ Cash
☐ Check
☐ Credit Card

For child care services from : ....
To : ....

Balance Due $: ....

Providers EIN Or SSN : ....

Providers Signature :

CHILD CARE RECEIPT

Child's Name : .... Date : ....

Received From : ....

Amount : $ [   ]

Paid By : ☐ Cash
☐ Check
☐ Credit Card

For child care services from : ....
To : ....

Balance Due $: ....

Providers EIN Or SSN : ....

Providers Signature :

CHILD CARE
RECEIPT

Child's Name : .... Date : ....

Received From : ....

Amount : $ [   ]

For child care services from : ....

Paid By : ☐ Cash
        ☐ Check
        ☐ Credit Card

To : ....

Balance Due $: ....

Providers EIN Or SSN : ....

Providers Signature :

CHILD CARE
RECEIPT

Child's Name : .... Date : ....

Received From : ....

Amount : $ [   ]

For child care services from : ....

Paid By : ☐ Cash
        ☐ Check
        ☐ Credit Card

To : ....

Balance Due $: ....

Providers EIN Or SSN : ....

Providers Signature :

CHILD CARE
RECEIPT

Child's Name : .... Date : ....

Received From : ....

Amount : $ [   ]

For child care services from : ....

Paid By : ☐ Cash
        ☐ Check
        ☐ Credit Card

To : ....

Balance Due $: ....

Providers EIN Or SSN : ....

Providers Signature :

CHILD CARE RECEIPT

Child's Name : .... Date : ....

Received From : ....

Amount : $ [   ]

Paid By : ☐ Cash
☐ Check
☐ Credit Card

For child care services from : ....
To : ....

Balance Due $: ....

Providers EIN Or SSN : ....

Providers Signature :

CHILD CARE RECEIPT

Child's Name : .... Date : ....

Received From : ....

Amount : $ [   ]

Paid By : ☐ Cash
☐ Check
☐ Credit Card

For child care services from : ....
To : ....

Balance Due $: ....

Providers EIN Or SSN : ....

Providers Signature :

CHILD CARE RECEIPT

Child's Name : .... Date : ....

Received From : ....

Amount : $ [   ]

Paid By : ☐ Cash
☐ Check
☐ Credit Card

For child care services from : ....
To : ....

Balance Due $: ....

Providers EIN Or SSN : ....

Providers Signature :

CHILD CARE RECEIPT

Child's Name : .... Date : ....

Received From : ....

Amount : $ _____

Paid By : ☐ Cash
☐ Check
☐ Credit Card

For child care services from : ....
To : ....

Balance Due $: ....

Providers EIN Or SSN : ....

Providers Signature :

CHILD CARE RECEIPT

Child's Name : .... Date : ....

Received From : ....

Amount : $ _____

Paid By : ☐ Cash
☐ Check
☐ Credit Card

For child care services from : ....
To : ....

Balance Due $: ....

Providers EIN Or SSN : ....

Providers Signature :

CHILD CARE RECEIPT

Child's Name : .... Date : ....

Received From : ....

Amount : $ _____

Paid By : ☐ Cash
☐ Check
☐ Credit Card

For child care services from : ....
To : ....

Balance Due $: ....

Providers EIN Or SSN : ....

Providers Signature :

CHILD CARE RECEIPT

Child's Name : ....   Date : ....

Received From : ....

Amount : $ [   ]

Paid By : ☐ Cash
☐ Check
☐ Credit Card

For child care services from : ....
To : ....

Balance Due $: ....

Providers EIN Or SSN : ....

Providers Signature :

CHILD CARE RECEIPT

Child's Name : ....   Date : ....

Received From : ....

Amount : $ [   ]

Paid By : ☐ Cash
☐ Check
☐ Credit Card

For child care services from : ....
To : ....

Balance Due $: ....

Providers EIN Or SSN : ....

Providers Signature :

CHILD CARE RECEIPT

Child's Name : ....   Date : ....

Received From : ....

Amount : $ [   ]

Paid By : ☐ Cash
☐ Check
☐ Credit Card

For child care services from : ....
To : ....

Balance Due $: ....

Providers EIN Or SSN : ....

Providers Signature :

CHILD CARE RECEIPT

Child's Name : ....   Date : ....

Received From : ....   Amount : $ [   ]

Paid By : ☐ Cash
For child care services from : ....   ☐ Check
To : ....   ☐ Credit Card
Balance Due $: ....
Providers EIN Or SSN : ....
Providers Signature :

CHILD CARE RECEIPT

Child's Name : ....   Date : ....

Received From : ....   Amount : $ [   ]

Paid By : ☐ Cash
For child care services from : ....   ☐ Check
To : ....   ☐ Credit Card
Balance Due $: ....
Providers EIN Or SSN : ....
Providers Signature :

CHILD CARE RECEIPT

Child's Name : ....   Date : ....

Received From : ....   Amount : $ [   ]

Paid By : ☐ Cash
For child care services from : ....   ☐ Check
To : ....   ☐ Credit Card
Balance Due $: ....
Providers EIN Or SSN : ....
Providers Signature :

CHILD CARE RECEIPT

Child's Name : .... Date : ....

Received From : ....

Amount : $ [   ]

Paid By : ☐ Cash
            ☐ Check
            ☐ Credit Card

For child care services from : ....
            To : ....

Balance Due $: ....

Providers EIN Or SSN : ....

Providers Signature :

CHILD CARE RECEIPT

Child's Name : .... Date : ....

Received From : ....

Amount : $ [   ]

Paid By : ☐ Cash
            ☐ Check
            ☐ Credit Card

For child care services from : ....
            To : ....

Balance Due $: ....

Providers EIN Or SSN : ....

Providers Signature :

CHILD CARE RECEIPT

Child's Name : .... Date : ....

Received From : ....

Amount : $ [   ]

Paid By : ☐ Cash
            ☐ Check
            ☐ Credit Card

For child care services from : ....
            To : ....

Balance Due $: ....

Providers EIN Or SSN : ....

Providers Signature :

CHILD CARE RECEIPT

Child's Name : .... Date : ....

Received From : ....

Amount : $ [ ]

Paid By : ☐ Cash
☐ Check
☐ Credit Card

For child care services from : ....
To : ....
Balance Due $: ....
Providers EIN Or SSN : ....

Providers Signature :

CHILD CARE RECEIPT

Child's Name : .... Date : ....

Received From : ....

Amount : $ [ ]

Paid By : ☐ Cash
☐ Check
☐ Credit Card

For child care services from : ....
To : ....
Balance Due $: ....
Providers EIN Or SSN : ....

Providers Signature :

CHILD CARE RECEIPT

Child's Name : .... Date : ....

Received From : ....

Amount : $ [ ]

Paid By : ☐ Cash
☐ Check
☐ Credit Card

For child care services from : ....
To : ....
Balance Due $: ....
Providers EIN Or SSN : ....

Providers Signature :

CHILD CARE RECEIPT

Child's Name : .... Date : ....

Received From : ....

Amount : $ _____

Paid By : ☐ Cash
☐ Check
☐ Credit Card

For child care services from : ....
To : ....

Balance Due $: ....

Providers EIN Or SSN : ....

Providers Signature :

CHILD CARE RECEIPT

Child's Name : .... Date : ....

Received From : ....

Amount : $ _____

Paid By : ☐ Cash
☐ Check
☐ Credit Card

For child care services from : ....
To : ....

Balance Due $: ....

Providers EIN Or SSN : ....

Providers Signature :

CHILD CARE RECEIPT

Child's Name : .... Date : ....

Received From : ....

Amount : $ _____

Paid By : ☐ Cash
☐ Check
☐ Credit Card

For child care services from : ....
To : ....

Balance Due $: ....

Providers EIN Or SSN : ....

Providers Signature :

CHILD CARE RECEIPT

Child's Name : .... Date : ....

Received From : .... Amount : $ _____

Paid By : ☐ Cash
For child care services from : .... ☐ Check
To : .... ☐ Credit Card
Balance Due $: ....
Providers EIN Or SSN : ....

Providers Signature :

CHILD CARE RECEIPT

Child's Name : .... Date : ....

Received From : .... Amount : $ _____

Paid By : ☐ Cash
For child care services from : .... ☐ Check
To : .... ☐ Credit Card
Balance Due $: ....
Providers EIN Or SSN : ....

Providers Signature :

CHILD CARE RECEIPT

Child's Name : .... Date : ....

Received From : .... Amount : $ _____

Paid By : ☐ Cash
For child care services from : .... ☐ Check
To : .... ☐ Credit Card
Balance Due $: ....
Providers EIN Or SSN : ....

Providers Signature :

CHILD CARE
RECEIPT

Child's Name : .... Date : ....

Received From : ....

Amount : $ [   ]

Paid By : ☐ Cash
☐ Check
☐ Credit Card

For child care services from : ....
To : ....

Balance Due $: ....

Providers EIN Or SSN : ....

Providers Signature : ....

CHILD CARE
RECEIPT

Child's Name : .... Date : ....

Received From : ....

Amount : $ [   ]

Paid By : ☐ Cash
☐ Check
☐ Credit Card

For child care services from : ....
To : ....

Balance Due $: ....

Providers EIN Or SSN : ....

Providers Signature : ....

CHILD CARE
RECEIPT

Child's Name : .... Date : ....

Received From : ....

Amount : $ [   ]

Paid By : ☐ Cash
☐ Check
☐ Credit Card

For child care services from : ....
To : ....

Balance Due $: ....

Providers EIN Or SSN : ....

Providers Signature : ....

CHILD CARE RECEIPT

Child's Name : ....   Date : ....

Received From : ....

Amount : $ [   ]

For child care services from : ....
To : ....

Paid By : ☐ Cash
☐ Check
☐ Credit Card

Balance Due $: ....

Providers EIN Or SSN : ....

Providers Signature :

CHILD CARE RECEIPT

Child's Name : ....   Date : ....

Received From : ....

Amount : $ [   ]

For child care services from : ....
To : ....

Paid By : ☐ Cash
☐ Check
☐ Credit Card

Balance Due $: ....

Providers EIN Or SSN : ....

Providers Signature :

CHILD CARE RECEIPT

Child's Name : ....   Date : ....

Received From : ....

Amount : $ [   ]

For child care services from : ....
To : ....

Paid By : ☐ Cash
☐ Check
☐ Credit Card

Balance Due $: ....

Providers EIN Or SSN : ....

Providers Signature :

CHILD CARE RECEIPT

Child's Name : .... Date : ....

Received From : ....

For child care services from : ....
To : ....

Balance Due $: ....

Providers EIN Or SSN : ....

Amount : $ _____

Paid By : ☐ Cash
☐ Check
☐ Credit Card

Providers Signature :

CHILD CARE RECEIPT

Child's Name : .... Date : ....

Received From : ....

For child care services from : ....
To : ....

Balance Due $: ....

Providers EIN Or SSN : ....

Amount : $ _____

Paid By : ☐ Cash
☐ Check
☐ Credit Card

Providers Signature :

CHILD CARE RECEIPT

Child's Name : .... Date : ....

Received From : ....

For child care services from : ....
To : ....

Balance Due $: ....

Providers EIN Or SSN : ....

Amount : $ _____

Paid By : ☐ Cash
☐ Check
☐ Credit Card

Providers Signature :

CHILD CARE RECEIPT

Child's Name : .... Date : ....

Received From : .... Amount : $ [   ]

For child care services from : .... Paid By : ☐ Cash
                          To : ....   ☐ Check
Balance Due $: ....   ☐ Credit Card
Providers EIN Or SSN : ....

Providers Signature :

CHILD CARE RECEIPT

Child's Name : .... Date : ....

Received From : .... Amount : $ [   ]

For child care services from : .... Paid By : ☐ Cash
                          To : ....   ☐ Check
Balance Due $: ....   ☐ Credit Card
Providers EIN Or SSN : ....

Providers Signature :

CHILD CARE RECEIPT

Child's Name : .... Date : ....

Received From : .... Amount : $ [   ]

For child care services from : .... Paid By : ☐ Cash
                          To : ....   ☐ Check
Balance Due $: ....   ☐ Credit Card
Providers EIN Or SSN : ....

Providers Signature :

CHILD CARE RECEIPT

Child's Name : .... Date : ....

Received From : ....

Amount : $ [   ]

Paid By : ☐ Cash
☐ Check
☐ Credit Card

For child care services from : ....
To : ....

Balance Due $: ....

Providers EIN Or SSN : ....

Providers Signature :

CHILD CARE RECEIPT

Child's Name : .... Date : ....

Received From : ....

Amount : $ [   ]

Paid By : ☐ Cash
☐ Check
☐ Credit Card

For child care services from : ....
To : ....

Balance Due $: ....

Providers EIN Or SSN : ....

Providers Signature :

CHILD CARE RECEIPT

Child's Name : .... Date : ....

Received From : ....

Amount : $ [   ]

Paid By : ☐ Cash
☐ Check
☐ Credit Card

For child care services from : ....
To : ....

Balance Due $: ....

Providers EIN Or SSN : ....

Providers Signature :

CHILD CARE RECEIPT

Child's Name : ....   Date : ....

Received From : ....   Amount : $ [   ]

Paid By : ☐ Cash
          ☐ Check
          ☐ Credit Card

For child care services from : ....
To : ....

Balance Due $: ....

Providers EIN Or SSN : ....

Providers Signature :

CHILD CARE RECEIPT

Child's Name : ....   Date : ....

Received From : ....   Amount : $ [   ]

Paid By : ☐ Cash
          ☐ Check
          ☐ Credit Card

For child care services from : ....
To : ....

Balance Due $: ....

Providers EIN Or SSN : ....

Providers Signature :

CHILD CARE RECEIPT

Child's Name : ....   Date : ....

Received From : ....   Amount : $ [   ]

Paid By : ☐ Cash
          ☐ Check
          ☐ Credit Card

For child care services from : ....
To : ....

Balance Due $: ....

Providers EIN Or SSN : ....

Providers Signature :

CHILD CARE RECEIPT

Child's Name : .... Date : ....

Received From : ....

Amount : $ _____

Paid By : ☐ Cash
☐ Check
☐ Credit Card

For child care services from : ....
To : ....

Balance Due $: ....

Providers EIN Or SSN : ....

Providers Signature :

CHILD CARE RECEIPT

Child's Name : .... Date : ....

Received From : ....

Amount : $ _____

Paid By : ☐ Cash
☐ Check
☐ Credit Card

For child care services from : ....
To : ....

Balance Due $: ....

Providers EIN Or SSN : ....

Providers Signature :

CHILD CARE RECEIPT

Child's Name : .... Date : ....

Received From : ....

Amount : $ _____

Paid By : ☐ Cash
☐ Check
☐ Credit Card

For child care services from : ....
To : ....

Balance Due $: ....

Providers EIN Or SSN : ....

Providers Signature :

CHILD CARE RECEIPT

Child's Name : ....   Date : ....

Received From : ....

For child care services from : ....

To : ....

Balance Due $: ....

Providers EIN Or SSN : ....

Amount : $ _____

Paid By : ☐ Cash
         ☐ Check
         ☐ Credit Card

Providers Signature :

CHILD CARE RECEIPT

Child's Name : ....   Date : ....

Received From : ....

For child care services from : ....

To : ....

Balance Due $: ....

Providers EIN Or SSN : ....

Amount : $ _____

Paid By : ☐ Cash
         ☐ Check
         ☐ Credit Card

Providers Signature :

CHILD CARE RECEIPT

Child's Name : ....   Date : ....

Received From : ....

For child care services from : ....

To : ....

Balance Due $: ....

Providers EIN Or SSN : ....

Amount : $ _____

Paid By : ☐ Cash
         ☐ Check
         ☐ Credit Card

Providers Signature :

CHILD CARE RECEIPT

Child's Name : .... Date : ....

Received From : ....

Amount : $ [   ]

For child care services from : ....

To : ....

Paid By : ☐ Cash
☐ Check
☐ Credit Card

Balance Due $: ....

Providers EIN Or SSN : ....

Providers Signature :

CHILD CARE RECEIPT

Child's Name : .... Date : ....

Received From : ....

Amount : $ [   ]

For child care services from : ....

To : ....

Paid By : ☐ Cash
☐ Check
☐ Credit Card

Balance Due $: ....

Providers EIN Or SSN : ....

Providers Signature :

CHILD CARE RECEIPT

Child's Name : .... Date : ....

Received From : ....

Amount : $ [   ]

For child care services from : ....

To : ....

Paid By : ☐ Cash
☐ Check
☐ Credit Card

Balance Due $: ....

Providers EIN Or SSN : ....

Providers Signature :

CHILD CARE
RECEIPT

Child's Name : .... Date : ....

Received From : ....

Amount : $ [   ]

Paid By : ☐ Cash
☐ Check
☐ Credit Card

For child care services from : ....
To : ....

Balance Due $: ....

Providers EIN Or SSN : ....

Providers Signature :

CHILD CARE
RECEIPT

Child's Name : .... Date : ....

Received From : ....

Amount : $ [   ]

Paid By : ☐ Cash
☐ Check
☐ Credit Card

For child care services from : ....
To : ....

Balance Due $: ....

Providers EIN Or SSN : ....

Providers Signature :

CHILD CARE
RECEIPT

Child's Name : .... Date : ....

Received From : ....

Amount : $ [   ]

Paid By : ☐ Cash
☐ Check
☐ Credit Card

For child care services from : ....
To : ....

Balance Due $: ....

Providers EIN Or SSN : ....

Providers Signature :

CHILD CARE RECEIPT

Child's Name : ....   Date : ....

Received From : ....

For child care services from : ....
To : ....
Balance Due $: ....
Providers EIN Or SSN : ....

Amount : $[   ]

Paid By : ☐ Cash
☐ Check
☐ Credit Card

Providers Signature :

CHILD CARE RECEIPT

Child's Name : ....   Date : ....

Received From : ....

For child care services from : ....
To : ....
Balance Due $: ....
Providers EIN Or SSN : ....

Amount : $[   ]

Paid By : ☐ Cash
☐ Check
☐ Credit Card

Providers Signature :

CHILD CARE RECEIPT

Child's Name : ....   Date : ....

Received From : ....

For child care services from : ....
To : ....
Balance Due $: ....
Providers EIN Or SSN : ....

Amount : $[   ]

Paid By : ☐ Cash
☐ Check
☐ Credit Card

Providers Signature :

CHILD CARE RECEIPT

Child's Name : .... Date : ....

Received From : ....

Amount : $ [   ]

Paid By : ☐ Cash
☐ Check
☐ Credit Card

For child care services from : ....
To : ....

Balance Due $: ....

Providers EIN Or SSN : ....

Providers Signature :

CHILD CARE RECEIPT

Child's Name : .... Date : ....

Received From : ....

Amount : $ [   ]

Paid By : ☐ Cash
☐ Check
☐ Credit Card

For child care services from : ....
To : ....

Balance Due $: ....

Providers EIN Or SSN : ....

Providers Signature :

CHILD CARE RECEIPT

Child's Name : .... Date : ....

Received From : ....

Amount : $ [   ]

Paid By : ☐ Cash
☐ Check
☐ Credit Card

For child care services from : ....
To : ....

Balance Due $: ....

Providers EIN Or SSN : ....

Providers Signature :

CHILD CARE RECEIPT

Child's Name : .... Date : ....

Received From : ....

Amount : $ _____

Paid By : ☐ Cash
☐ Check
☐ Credit Card

For child care services from : ....
To : ....

Balance Due $: ....

Providers EIN Or SSN : ....

Providers Signature :

CHILD CARE RECEIPT

Child's Name : .... Date : ....

Received From : ....

Amount : $ _____

Paid By : ☐ Cash
☐ Check
☐ Credit Card

For child care services from : ....
To : ....

Balance Due $: ....

Providers EIN Or SSN : ....

Providers Signature :

CHILD CARE RECEIPT

Child's Name : .... Date : ....

Received From : ....

Amount : $ _____

Paid By : ☐ Cash
☐ Check
☐ Credit Card

For child care services from : ....
To : ....

Balance Due $: ....

Providers EIN Or SSN : ....

Providers Signature :

CHILD CARE RECEIPT

Child's Name : .... Date : ....

Received From : ....

For child care services from : ....
To : ....
Balance Due $: ....
Providers EIN Or SSN : ....

Amount : $ [   ]

Paid By : ☐ Cash
           ☐ Check
           ☐ Credit Card

Providers Signature :

CHILD CARE RECEIPT

Child's Name : .... Date : ....

Received From : ....

For child care services from : ....
To : ....
Balance Due $: ....
Providers EIN Or SSN : ....

Amount : $ [   ]

Paid By : ☐ Cash
           ☐ Check
           ☐ Credit Card

Providers Signature :

CHILD CARE RECEIPT

Child's Name : .... Date : ....

Received From : ....

For child care services from : ....
To : ....
Balance Due $: ....
Providers EIN Or SSN : ....

Amount : $ [   ]

Paid By : ☐ Cash
           ☐ Check
           ☐ Credit Card

Providers Signature :

CHILD CARE RECEIPT

Child's Name : .... Date : ....

Received From : ....

Amount : $☐

Paid By : ☐ Cash
          ☐ Check
          ☐ Credit Card

For child care services from : ....
To : ....

Balance Due $: ....

Providers EIN Or SSN : ....

Providers Signature :

CHILD CARE RECEIPT

Child's Name : .... Date : ....

Received From : ....

Amount : $☐

Paid By : ☐ Cash
          ☐ Check
          ☐ Credit Card

For child care services from : ....
To : ....

Balance Due $: ....

Providers EIN Or SSN : ....

Providers Signature :

CHILD CARE RECEIPT

Child's Name : .... Date : ....

Received From : ....

Amount : $☐

Paid By : ☐ Cash
          ☐ Check
          ☐ Credit Card

For child care services from : ....
To : ....

Balance Due $: ....

Providers EIN Or SSN : ....

Providers Signature :

CHILD CARE
RECEIPT

Child's Name : ....   Date : ....

Received From : ....

Amount : $ [____]

Paid By : ☐ Cash
              ☐ Check
              ☐ Credit Card

For child care services from : ....
           To : ....

Balance Due $: ....

Providers EIN Or SSN : ....

Providers Signature :

CHILD CARE
RECEIPT

Child's Name : ....   Date : ....

Received From : ....

Amount : $ [____]

Paid By : ☐ Cash
              ☐ Check
              ☐ Credit Card

For child care services from : ....
           To : ....

Balance Due $: ....

Providers EIN Or SSN : ....

Providers Signature :

CHILD CARE
RECEIPT

Child's Name : ....   Date : ....

Received From : ....

Amount : $ [____]

Paid By : ☐ Cash
              ☐ Check
              ☐ Credit Card

For child care services from : ....
           To : ....

Balance Due $: ....

Providers EIN Or SSN : ....

Providers Signature :

CHILD CARE RECEIPT

Child's Name : .... Date : ....

Received From : ....

Amount : $ [   ]

For child care services from : ....
To : ....

Paid By : ☐ Cash
☐ Check
☐ Credit Card

Balance Due $: ....

Providers EIN Or SSN : ....

Providers Signature :

CHILD CARE RECEIPT

Child's Name : .... Date : ....

Received From : ....

Amount : $ [   ]

For child care services from : ....
To : ....

Paid By : ☐ Cash
☐ Check
☐ Credit Card

Balance Due $: ....

Providers EIN Or SSN : ....

Providers Signature :

CHILD CARE RECEIPT

Child's Name : .... Date : ....

Received From : ....

Amount : $ [   ]

For child care services from : ....
To : ....

Paid By : ☐ Cash
☐ Check
☐ Credit Card

Balance Due $: ....

Providers EIN Or SSN : ....

Providers Signature :

CHILD CARE RECEIPT

Child's Name : .... Date : ....

Received From : ....

Amount : $ [   ]

Paid By : ☐ Cash
☐ Check
☐ Credit Card

For child care services from : ....
To : ....
Balance Due $: ....
Providers EIN Or SSN : ....

Providers Signature :

CHILD CARE RECEIPT

Child's Name : .... Date : ....

Received From : ....

Amount : $ [   ]

Paid By : ☐ Cash
☐ Check
☐ Credit Card

For child care services from : ....
To : ....
Balance Due $: ....
Providers EIN Or SSN : ....

Providers Signature :

CHILD CARE RECEIPT

Child's Name : .... Date : ....

Received From : ....

Amount : $ [   ]

Paid By : ☐ Cash
☐ Check
☐ Credit Card

For child care services from : ....
To : ....
Balance Due $: ....
Providers EIN Or SSN : ....

Providers Signature :

CHILD CARE RECEIPT

Child's Name : .... Date : ....

Received From : ....

Amount : $ _____

Paid By : ☐ Cash
☐ Check
☐ Credit Card

For child care services from : ....
To : ....

Balance Due $: ....

Providers EIN Or SSN : ....

Providers Signature :

CHILD CARE RECEIPT

Child's Name : .... Date : ....

Received From : ....

Amount : $ _____

Paid By : ☐ Cash
☐ Check
☐ Credit Card

For child care services from : ....
To : ....

Balance Due $: ....

Providers EIN Or SSN : ....

Providers Signature :

CHILD CARE RECEIPT

Child's Name : .... Date : ....

Received From : ....

Amount : $ _____

Paid By : ☐ Cash
☐ Check
☐ Credit Card

For child care services from : ....
To : ....

Balance Due $: ....

Providers EIN Or SSN : ....

Providers Signature :

CHILD CARE
RECEIPT

Child's Name : .... Date : ....

Received From : ....

Amount : $ [   ]

Paid By : ☐ Cash
          ☐ Check
          ☐ Credit Card

For child care services from : ....
                          To : ....
Balance Due $: ....
Providers EIN Or SSN : ....
                    Providers Signature :

CHILD CARE
RECEIPT

Child's Name : .... Date : ....

Received From : ....

Amount : $ [   ]

Paid By : ☐ Cash
          ☐ Check
          ☐ Credit Card

For child care services from : ....
                          To : ....
Balance Due $: ....
Providers EIN Or SSN : ....
                    Providers Signature :

CHILD CARE
RECEIPT

Child's Name : .... Date : ....

Received From : ....

Amount : $ [   ]

Paid By : ☐ Cash
          ☐ Check
          ☐ Credit Card

For child care services from : ....
                          To : ....
Balance Due $: ....
Providers EIN Or SSN : ....
                    Providers Signature :

CHILD CARE RECEIPT

Child's Name : .... Date : ....

Received From : ....

Amount : $ [   ]

Paid By : ☐ Cash
           ☐ Check
           ☐ Credit Card

For child care services from : ....
         To : ....

Balance Due $: ....
Providers EIN Or SSN : ....

Providers Signature :

CHILD CARE RECEIPT

Child's Name : .... Date : ....

Received From : ....

Amount : $ [   ]

Paid By : ☐ Cash
           ☐ Check
           ☐ Credit Card

For child care services from : ....
         To : ....

Balance Due $: ....
Providers EIN Or SSN : ....

Providers Signature :

CHILD CARE RECEIPT

Child's Name : .... Date : ....

Received From : ....

Amount : $ [   ]

Paid By : ☐ Cash
           ☐ Check
           ☐ Credit Card

For child care services from : ....
         To : ....

Balance Due $: ....
Providers EIN Or SSN : ....

Providers Signature :

CHILD CARE RECEIPT

Child's Name : .... Date : ....

Received From : .... Amount : $ [   ]

For child care services from : .... Paid By : ☐ Cash
                         To : ....   ☐ Check
Balance Due $: ....   ☐ Credit Card
Providers EIN Or SSN : ....
                    Providers Signature :

CHILD CARE RECEIPT

Child's Name : .... Date : ....

Received From : .... Amount : $ [   ]

For child care services from : .... Paid By : ☐ Cash
                         To : ....   ☐ Check
Balance Due $: ....   ☐ Credit Card
Providers EIN Or SSN : ....
                    Providers Signature :

CHILD CARE RECEIPT

Child's Name : .... Date : ....

Received From : .... Amount : $ [   ]

For child care services from : .... Paid By : ☐ Cash
                         To : ....   ☐ Check
Balance Due $: ....   ☐ Credit Card
Providers EIN Or SSN : ....
                    Providers Signature :

CHILD CARE RECEIPT

Child's Name : .... Date : ....

Received From : ....

Amount : $ [   ]

Paid By : ☐ Cash
☐ Check
☐ Credit Card

For child care services from : ....
To : ....

Balance Due $: ....

Providers EIN Or SSN : ....

Providers Signature :

CHILD CARE RECEIPT

Child's Name : .... Date : ....

Received From : ....

Amount : $ [   ]

Paid By : ☐ Cash
☐ Check
☐ Credit Card

For child care services from : ....
To : ....

Balance Due $: ....

Providers EIN Or SSN : ....

Providers Signature :

CHILD CARE RECEIPT

Child's Name : .... Date : ....

Received From : ....

Amount : $ [   ]

Paid By : ☐ Cash
☐ Check
☐ Credit Card

For child care services from : ....
To : ....

Balance Due $: ....

Providers EIN Or SSN : ....

Providers Signature :

Made in the USA
Middletown, DE
21 July 2023

35536512R00057